C000134024

Zen Vows for Daily Life

Robert Aitken

Wisdom

Wisdom Publications
199 Elm Street
Somerville, MA 02144 USA
wisdompubs.org

Library of Congress Cataloging-in-Publication Data
Names: Aitken, Robert, 1917–2010, author.
Title: Zen vows for daily life / Robert Aitken.
Description: First Wisdom edition. | Somerville, MA: Wisdom
Publications, 2018. | Originally published: Berkeley,
Calif.: Parallax Press, 1992. | Includes index. |
Identifiers: LCCN 2017018210 (print) | LCCN 2018001538 (ebook) |
ISBN 9781614294016 (ebook) | ISBN 1614294011 (ebook) |
ISBN 9781614293859 (hardcover: alk. paper) |
ISBN 1614293856 (hardcover: alk. paper)
Subjects: LCSH: Zen Buddhism—Prayers and
devotions. | Zen meditations.
Classification: LCC BQ9289.5 (ebook) | LCC BQ9289.5 .A35 2018
(print) | DDC 294.3/443—dc23
LC record available at https://lccn.loc.gov/2017018210

ISBN 978-1-61429-385-9   ebook ISBN 978-1-61429-401-6

22 21 20 19 18
5 4 3 2 1

Cover design by Phil Pascuzzo. Interior design by
Gopa & Ted2, Inc. Set in Adobe Garmond Pro 11/15.

Wisdom Publications' books are printed on acid-free paper and meet
the guidelines for permanence and durability of the Production
Guidelines for Book Longevity of the Council on Library Resources.

Printed in China

To my parents and grandparents:
Gladys Baker and Robert Thomas Aitken,
Jessie Thomas and Robert Grant Aitken,

and

Florence Page and James Bartlett Baker—
who bred ethics into my bones.

My heart was full; I made no vows, but vows
Were then made for me.

WORDSWORTH
The Prelude

Foreword

When I entered the monastery as a novice, the first book I studied was *Gathas for Everyday Life*, compiled by the Chinese Zen master Du Ti. Gathas are short verses we can recite during the day to help us dwell in mindfulness and look more deeply at what we are doing. Today I still practice many of the gathas from that book—when I wake up, when I put on my shoes, when I wash the dishes, when I enter the meditation hall. I have even compiled a handbook of forty-nine gathas to use for practicing in modern times.

In 1985, I met Robert Aitken, roshi at his zendo in Hawaii, and I was pleased to discover that he is a poet who deeply appreciates practicing with gathas. In the Zen tradition, poetry and meditation always go together. In China, Japan, Korea, and Vietnam, everyone likes poetry, and we use poetry to make the practice of meditation enjoyable. Poetry is comprised of images and music, and images make the practice easy.

In this book, Aitken Roshi offers us many beautiful verses that we can use to reflect more deeply on what we are doing. What is going on is very important. Life in society is complex, and it is easy to lose ourselves in regrets about the past or anxieties about the future. The only moment we can be alive is this moment, and gathas, simple verses that state our intention to dwell in mindfulness, can bring us back to life. If we only dwell in the past or the future, we are like a ghost, and if our little boy or girl comes up to us and presents us with a beautiful smile, we will miss it. What a pity!

Practicing mindfulness with gathas helps us develop concentration. In Buddhism, meditation means looking deeply into the heart of reality, and concentration is the basic condition for this practice. In itself, concentration contains the seeds of the kind of insight that frees us from afflictions and reveals to us the nature of reality.

I hope this book will inspire many readers to continue the Zen tradition of using verses to better enjoy daily life and cultivate concentration and insight. I hope you will use Aitken Roshi's verses throughout the day and that one day you will begin to compose and practice with your own gathas as well. Don't try to use too many at once. Start with one or two or three or four, and memorize them. Then, when the occasion for using your verse arises, you will be ready. We must keep the practice relevant and up-to-date, and *Zen Vows for Daily Life* is a sterling example of this. I am grateful to Aitken Roshi for offering us this beautiful book.

Thich Nhat Hanh
Plum Village

Introduction

The poems in this book set forth occasions for religious practice. Though I made them for modern students, I was inspired by antique antecedents, back to the historical Buddha. My purpose in this essay is to present the ideas and forms of those antecedents.

The Buddha's original teaching is essentially a matter of four points—the four noble truths:

1. Anguish is everywhere.
2. We desire permanent existence for ourselves and for our loved ones, and we desire to prove ourselves independent of others and superior to them. These desires conflict with the way things are: nothing abides, and everything and everyone depends upon everything and everyone else. This conflict causes our anguish, and we project this anguish on those we meet.
3. Release from anguish comes with the personal acknowledgment and resolve: we are here together

very briefly, so let us accept reality fully and take care of one another while we can.

4. This acknowledgment and resolve are realized by following the eightfold path: right views, right thinking, right speech, right conduct, right livelihood, right effort, right recollection, and right meditation. Here *right* means "correct"or "accurate"—in keeping with the reality of impermanence and interdependence.[1]

The four noble truths are called "noble" because they present the vocation of wisdom and compassion. They are the foundation of all Buddhism, and form the heart of modern-day Theravada, the Buddhism of South and Southeast Asia.

Mahayana, a later tradition that became the Buddhism of East Asia, produced quite radical changes in the way those basic ideas were interpreted and expressed. For example, early emphasis was upon demonstrating the insubstantial nature of the self, but in the Mahayana that insubstantial essence itself is given attention:

It shines everywhere in the daily activities of everyone, appearing in everything. Though you try to grasp it, you cannot get it; though you try to abandon it, it always remains. It is vast and unobstructed, utterly empty.[2]

As to interdependence, the Mahayana Buddhist finds that relationships are not just the ordinary activity of giving and receiving support, but in every situation the other person, animal, plant, or thing is experienced as oneself. This is "interbeing," to use Thich Nhat Hanh's felicitous term, and is presented vividly in a multitude of expansive and profound metaphors in the *Avatamsaka Sutra*, translated into Chinese as the *Hua-yen ching*, the last great chronicle of the Mahayana. Central among these metaphors is "The Net of Indra": a multidimensional net of all beings (including inanimate things), with each point, each knot, a jewel that perfectly reflects, and indeed contains, all other points.[3] This cosmic yet intimate perspective is offered again and again throughout the sutra. Thomas Cleary, scholar of Hua-yen philosophy, writes:

All things [are interdependent, and] therefore imply in their individual being the simultaneous being of all other things.

Thus it is said that the existence of each element of the universe includes the existence of the whole universe and hence is as extensive as the universe itself.[4]

This is philosophy at its grandest, and the Buddhist is left with the task of making it personal. Religions with Near Eastern antecedents permit a personal relationship with God, and while many of the metaphorical figures in the *Hua-yen ching* could be called deities, there is no single God ruling all. The Buddha's followers cannot pray, "Thy kingdom come, Thy will be done," but instead they have made such formal promises as, "I will awaken my mind to the teachings of the Buddha for the benefit of all beings." Such vows are found in the very earliest Buddhist writings and continue to be of primary importance as a way of personalizing the practice in all forms of the religion today.[5]

In addition to vows, another way to personalize the Buddha's teaching has been to repeat gathas, four-line verses that sum up important points. Gathas too are found in the earliest Buddhist writings, and commonly have been memorized and used for right recollection—guideposts on the Buddha's path. *The Dhammapada*, an anthology drawn from early Buddhist texts, consists entirely of gathas, some of them probably dating from the Buddha's own time. Here is one that is known throughout the various streams of Buddhism today:

> Renounce all evil;
> practice all good;
> keep your mind pure;
> thus all the Buddhas taught.[6]

As Buddhism evolved, we find gathas and vows evolving as well. Early followers vowed to practice wisdom and compassion so that everyone and everything could thereby be freed from anguish. Their successors also vow to engage in wisdom and compassion, but *with*, rather than for, everyone and everything. This is called the way of the bodhisattva, "the enlightening being."[7]

Certain traditional bodhisattvas like Kuan-yin are venerated and even worshiped for the power of the vows they have taken to save everyone and everything. However, Mahayana teachers are clear that the bodhisattva is an archetype rather than a deity. When I take the noble path of the Buddha, the bodhisattva is no other than my selfless self. The bodhisattva vows are my own.[8]

In the Mahayana the two forms of vows and gathas often converge. The *Hua-yen ching* includes a chapter called "Purifying Practice," consisting of 139 gatha-vows, and I have followed their form in composing the poems in this book. The first line establishes the occasion, the second line presents the act of vowing, and the last two lines follow through with the specific conduct that one promises to undertake in these circumstances.

For example, here is a gatha from the "Purifying Practice" chapter:

> When I see flowing water
>   I vow with all beings
> to develop a wholesome will
> and wash away the stains of delusion.[9]

As always, translation is problematic. Word-for-word the Chinese original reads:

> If see flow water
>   then vow all beings
> gain good intention desire
> cleanse dispel delusion dirt.[10]

The second line is the same in all the *Hua-yen* gathas, and its wording is crucial. The translator must choose a pronoun to indicate who is vowing, and also a word to connect "vow" with the rest of the poem. Cleary translates the line, "They should wish that all beings. . . ."[11] "They" are bodhisattvas, a reference back to the introductory part of the chapter, where Manjushri is asked an elaborate, lengthy question about how bodhisattvas can attain wisdom and compassion. He replies with the 139 gathas that set forth occasions to follow the Buddha Way.[12]

We ourselves are bodhisattvas, so we make these gathas our own. The translation, "They should vow that all beings / develop a wholesome will" becomes "I vow with all beings / to develop a wholesome will." I myself follow the eightfold path and I join everyone and everything in turning the wheel of the Dharma toward universal understanding. I vow to use the many events of my day as opportunities to fulfill the task I share with all people, animals, plants, and things. Such vows take *ahimsa*, or non-harming, to the most profound level of personal responsibility. I might not realize them completely, but I do the best I can.

Making the vows my own is in keeping with

the innermost purpose of Mahayana practice, especially Zen practice. I make the reality of the Buddha's teaching my own. We are here only briefly and we depend on each other—this reality is my own. Even more personally: "This very body is the Buddha," as Hakuin Zenji declared.[13] This is my truth, told of my own body, spoken for me. Everything is affected each time I make a move, here in the grand net of the universe, and as I rediscover my own Buddha nature, my vows are naturally the vows of the Buddha that all beings be freed from their anguish.

"I vow with all beings" is my compassionate vow: "I vow, and I yearn that all beings might vow with me." It is my invitation that we enter the noble way together. It is also my affirmation of the Buddha's wise teaching of harmony: "I vow, and with universal affinities uniting everyone and everything, all beings are joining me as I vow." Compassion and wisdom thus blend and are one as I repeat, "I vow with all beings."

It is a noble yet everyday-life practice. Events set forth in *Hua-yen* gathas follow the routine of T'ang period monks and nuns. Each act in the monastery —washing up, putting on clothes, entering the

Buddha hall, sitting down for meditation, getting up from meditation—receives its Dharma poem. Events on pilgrimage—encountering a tree, a river, a bridge, a dignitary, a mendicant—likewise offer entries into the truth. My purpose in this book is similar: to show how ordinary occurrences in our modern lay life are in fact the Buddha's own teachings, and also to show how we can involve ourselves accordingly in the practice of wisdom and compassion with family and friends—with everyone and everything.

Of course, monks and nuns of the T'ang period had no gathas for noticing a billboard advertising Jim Beam Kentucky Sour Mash Whiskey. As lay Western Buddhists, however, we pick our way daily through an agglomeration of compelling reminders to pamper ourselves and serve no one else. Our task is harder, it seems, than the one that faced our ancestors. Somehow we must cultivate methods, perhaps including gathas, to follow the noble path of the Buddha as fellow citizens of Jim Beam and his acquisitive cohorts.

Formal meditation for twenty-five minutes or so per day, meditation meetings once or twice a week, and periodic retreats—all are helpful methods.

Most of us do not, however, live in temples, with their moment-to-moment invitations to religious practice. We are caught up in the accelerating tempo of earning a living, and right recollection tends to disappear except during times of formal meditation.

Moreover, we in the modern Western world are children of Freud as well as of the Buddha. Classical gathas do not deal with human relationships or emotions, just as the Japanese haiku form of poetry leaves that side of life alone. I find myself wanting gathas that show the way to practice and realize interbeing when I am angry with someone. I want gathas of impermanence when my plans don't work out. What do I do if I am made to wait for someone? How should I respond to an offer of meaningless sex?

Accordingly, I find that many of my gathas are rather like *senryu*, the Japanese poetical form that uses the same syllabic count and line arrangement as haiku. Senryu verses deal with parents, spouses, children, in-laws, neighbors, work supervisors, economics, and politics. The metaphors are as complex as the situations, full of irony and satire.[14] This is human life, which I want my gathas to address.

Finally, gathas must be reckoned as poetry, and in this respect the classical gathas are rather thin. I don't find much ambiguity, irony, paradox, doubt, humor, playfulness, chance, absurdity, frustration, or mystery in them.

However, they inspire my practice (including my writing), and for the devotional occasions of stepping into the meditation hall, bowing, reciting sutras, and settling down for zazen, I hope that my gathas will tend for the most part to be as straightforward and simple-hearted as my models.

I have confined diacritical marks to the reference portions of the book, except for a couple of cases where an accent seems necessary for correct pronunciation.

Notes

1. Walpola Rahula, *What the Buddha Taught* (New York: Grove Press, 1974), 16–50.
2. Christopher Cleary, trans., *Swampland Flowers: The Letters and Lectures of the Zen Master Ta Hui* (New York: Grove Press, 1977), 34.
3. Thomas Cleary, *Entry into the Inconceivable: An Introduction to Hua-yen Buddhism* (Honolulu: University of Hawaii Press, 1983), 37.
4. Ibid., 7.

5. Har Dayal, *The Bodhisattva Doctrine in Buddhist Sanskrit Literature* (London: Kegan Paul, 1931), 65.

6. Cf. Irving Babbitt, trans., *The Dhammapada* (New York: New Directions, 1965), 30.

7. Thomas Cleary, trans., *The Flower Ornament Scripture: A Translation of the Avatamsaka Sutra*, 3 vols. (Boulder and London: Shambhala, 1984–87), 2:16–17.

8. The monk Nyogen Senzaki used to address his American students, "Bodhisattvas," the way speakers of his time would begin their talks, "Ladies and Gentlemen." See also ibid., 1:312–13.

9. Cf. Cleary, *The Flower Ornament Scripture*, 1:321.

10. For the original Chinese see *Flower Adornment Sutra*, ed. by Hsiian Hua, multiple volumes in process, chapter 11, *Pure Conduct*, trans. by Heng Tsai et al. (Talmage, CA: Dharma Realm Buddhist University, 1982), 171.

11. Cleary, *The Flower Ornament Scripture*, 1:321.

12. Ibid., 1:313–29.

13. Hakuin Ekaku, *Zazen Wasan* ("Song of Zazen"), in Robert Aitken, trans., *Taking the Path of Zen* (San Francisco: North Point Press, 1982), 113.

14. R. H. Blyth, "Haiku and Senryu," in *Senryu: Japanese Satirical Verses* (Tokyo: Hokuseido Press, 1949), 12–47.

The Gathas

Waking up in the morning
    I vow with all beings
to be ready for sparks of the Dharma
from flowers or children or birds.

———

Waking up in the morning
    I vow with all beings
to listen to those whom I love,
especially to things they don't say.

———

Watching the sky before dawn
    I vow with all beings
to open those flawless eyes
that welcomed the Morning Star.

Preparing to enter the shower
　　I vow with all beings
to wash off the last residue
of thoughts about being pure.

———

Preparing to enter the shower
　　I vow with all beings
to cleanse this body of Buddha
and go naked into the world.

———

Turning to use the toilet
　　I vow with all beings
to honor my body's knowledge
of what to retain and discard.

Lathering up for a shave
     I vow with all beings
to cut off my silly vanity
and trust what is there underneath.

———

When I check my face in the mirror
     I vow with all beings
to present the original woman
who preceded the Buddha-Tao.

———

Though revisions appeared in the night
     I vow with all beings:
first water the plants in the bathroom
then give the dishes their turn.

Lighting a candle for Buddha,
    I vow with all beings
to honor your clear affirmation:
"Forget yourself and you're free."

———

Offering flowers to Buddha
    I vow with all beings
to honor your loving compassion
for those of us just serving time.

———

Offering incense to Buddha
    I vow with all beings
to honor your keen nose for concepts
and your vigor in smiting them all.

Offering water to Buddha
      I vow with all beings
to honor your fathomless wellspring,
sustaining great life and great death.

———

Offering rice to the Buddha
      I vow with all beings
to honor your gentle injunction
that we keep our sustenance plain.

———

Sounding a bell at the temple
      I vow with all beings
to ring as true in each moment:
mellow, steady, and clear.

Sounding a bell at the temple
   I vow with all beings
to remember I'm ringing the Dharma
for the Sangha of all who can hear.

———

With the sound of the temple bell
   I vow with all beings
to offer my skull as a bell
in the echoing chiliocosms.

———

Beginning our sutra service
   I vow with all beings
to join my voice with all voices
and give life to each word as it comes.

Turning for refuge in Buddha
     I vow with all beings
to walk past pure and impure
straight down the Middle Way.

———

Turning for refuge in Dharma
     I vow with all beings
to oil and sharpen my tools
and fashion a home of the Tao.

———

Turning for refuge in Sangha
     I vow with all beings
to open myself to the geckos
and the strange behavior of friends.

With tea at the start of our sesshin
　　I vow with all beings
to let each breath hold my koan,
each bell be a call to return.

———

Taking my seat in the Zendo
　　I vow with all beings
to acknowledge that here is the sacred:
this bottom, this body, this breath.

———

When I sit in the interview line
　　I vow with all beings
to turn my face to my koan
and forget my scenarios.

When I enter the interview room
    I vow with all beings
to trust my innate gumption
and simply say it or do it.

———

As one who enjoys explication
    I vow with all beings
to leave out meaning completely
heart-to-heart in the interview room.

———

Coming back from the interview room
    I vow with all beings
to sink to the point of my koan
and let my conjecturing go.

When I enter the Zendo and bow
    I vow with all beings
to dance the dream of the Buddha
with my friends once again.

———

When I bow to the floor before Buddha
    I vow with all beings
to release my needless fixations
and die to myself at last.

———

When I bow to my sisters and brothers
    I vow with all beings
to freshen our intimate kinship
and enliven the practice we share.

When I bow to my sisters and brothers
    I vow with all beings
to include my sisters and brothers
from old who sit with us here.

———

When I sit with my friends in zazen
    I vow with all beings
to touch and receive and convey
the mind of rivers and stars.

———

Sitting alone in zazen
    I vow with all beings
to remember I'm sitting together
with mountains, children, and bears.

When I bow at the end of zazen
    I vow with all beings
to practice this intimate lightness
with family and friends and myself.

———

Holding hands in a ring
    I vow with all beings
to ease the pain in the ring
of breath around the world.

———

When joining others for sharing
    I vow with all beings
to give my report on the weather
without making a mess on the floor.

At a Zendo meeting for business
    I vow with all beings
to drop my plan in the hopper
and let the process evolve.

———

When the meeting gets loud and contentious
    I vow with all beings
to hold fast to my breath as a tiller
and take each wave as it comes.

———

When I come to the temple on workday
    I vow with all beings
to take up my hammer and paintbrush
as Samantabhadra's sword.

When someone brings me a flower
    I vow with all beings
to renew my practice of Dana,
the gift, the way to begin.

———

When someone rolls up in a wheelchair
    I vow with all beings
to welcome this cogent teacher
of life that's fashioned from death.

———

When women say I am sexist
    I vow with all beings
to ask for specific examples
and give them a chance to sink in.

Whenever I'm tempted to smoke
    I vow with all beings
to respect the marvelous process
of air transmuting to blood.

———

When someone offers a drink
    I vow with all beings
to acknowledge the sorrow it causes
while it warms and gladdens our hearts.

———

When someone lights up a number
    I vow with all beings
to point out its karmic connection
with paranoid stealth in the night.

When a question threatens my thesis
    I vow with all beings
to try it out as antithesis
and see if a synthesis works.

————

When people show anger and malice
    I vow with all beings
to listen for truth in the message,
ignoring the way it is said.

————

Whenever I'm feeling imposed on
    I vow with all beings
to recall that interdependence
means for others the other is me.

When I'm worried about my attachments
    I vow with all beings
to remember interdependence:
if I weren't attached I'd be dead.

———

When I'm worried about my condition
    I vow with all beings
to rest in my human condition:
breathing in, breathing out, heart beat.

———

When I'm worried about my condition
    I vow with all beings
to recall good and bad are conditions
that pollute our clear mountain stream.

Feeling toxic with aches in my joints
     I vow with all beings
to acknowledge we're all of us dying
and take comfort in hot lemonade.

———

When the doctor pokes here and there
     I vow with all beings
to concede that my cellular structure
will all come apart soon enough.

———

When the dentist takes up his drill
     I vow with all beings
to welcome the pain and discomfort
as doors to a steady mind.

Watching my body get older
 I vow with all beings
to be absolute for dying
and rejoice in my family and friends.

———

Facing my imminent death
 I vow with all beings
to go with the natural process,
at peace with whatever comes.

———

When someone close to me dies
 I vow with all beings
to settle in ultimate closeness
and continue our dialogue there.

When it's hard to be true to my faith
    I vow with all beings
to trust that my little hobgoblin
will find ways to help me hold fast.

———

When the outcome proves disappointing
    I vow with all beings
to look again at my purpose—
was it Dharma or something else?

———

In dealing with questions of sex
    I vow with all beings
to recall the perennial precepts:
"Don't harm, don't steal, don't exploit."

Embracing my lover in bed
        I vow with all beings
to bring patience and care and the joy
of new life to our ancient dance.

———

In the midst of thunder and lightning
        I vow with all beings
to enter the game with my children—
"One, two, three, *boom!*"

———

Walking my baby at night
        I vow with all beings
to give rest and space and time
and a chance to my child and all children.

When I powder my baby's bottom
    I vow with all beings
to freshen my innocent senses
and jingle the toys of the mind.

———

When the children get cranky and whiny
    I vow with all beings
to stop what I'm doing and cuddle
and show them I know times are tough.

———

When the children fight in the car
    I vow with all beings
to show how the car doesn't move
unless all of its parts are engaged.

When I turn into somebody nasty
    I vow with all beings
to reflect on how it all happened
and uncover my long-hidden tail.

———

When I'm moved to complain about others
    I vow with all beings
to remember that karma is endless
and it's loving that leads to love.

———

When I panic at losing my bearings
    I vow with all beings
to acknowledge the error is panic,
not losing familiar ground.

Kicking a chair in the dark
    I vow with all beings
to let the pain and surprise
slow me down to this step, this step.

———

When beset by personal problems
    I vow with all beings
to settle myself in zazen
and trust the path to come clear.

———

When beset by personal problems
    I vow with all beings
to return to my practice of patience—
"All things pass quickly away."

When beset by personal problems
    I vow with all beings
to recall the Perfection of Patience:
the ease of stars and the moon.

———

When my efforts are clearly outclassed
    I vow with all beings
to face my own limitations
and bring forth my original self.

———

When things fall apart on the job
    I vow with all beings
to use this regretful energy
and pick up the pieces with care.

When I find I've let people down
    I vow with all beings
to use this remorseful energy
and not get down on myself.

———

Whenever I'm down on myself
    I vow with all beings
to smile at my shallow concerns—
I'm not yet touching the ground.

———

When something precious gets stolen
    I vow with all beings
to acknowledge that soon I'll release
all things to the king of thieves.

When everything loses its meaning
　I vow with all beings
to honor this intimate teaching
that clears my dependence away.

———

Whenever I feel nothing matters
　I vow with all beings
to look in at my sleeping children
and murmur my vows again.

———

Whenever my vows seem meaningless
　I vow with all beings
to recall my original purpose,
boot up, and get with it again.

When I'm frazzled with anticipation
    I vow with all beings
to enjoy a long hot bath
and a record of Josquin des Prés.

———

When I look at the various options,
    I vow with all beings
to extinguish my wayward conjectures
and let my toes be my guide.

———

When wayward thoughts are persistent
    I vow with all beings
to imagine that even the Buddha
had silly ideas sometimes.

When wayward thoughts are persistent
  I vow with all beings
to release a Grandmother sigh—
stop on Mu, really stop.

———

When thoughts form an endless procession,
  I vow with all beings
to notice the spaces between them
and give the thrushes a chance.

———

In a paranoid cycle of thoughts
  I vow with all beings
to enjoy a cold glass of water
and step out to look at the sky.

When my head is a turmoil of trivia
    I vow with all beings
to relax in good-humored patience
as I would with a mischievous child.

———

When amused by thoughts in zazen
    I vow with all beings
to wave them through with a smile
and not follow them out the door.

———

When a demon disrupts my zazen
    I vow with all beings
to explain I'm busy right now,
we'll work things out later on.

When a demon disrupts my zazen
    I vow with all beings
to remember who generates demons
and return with a smile to my breath.

———

When the point of my koan eludes me
    I vow with all beings
to remember how linnets appear
when I fill up their feeder and wait.

———

In agony over my koan
    I vow with all beings
to give up and refer it along
to the dragon who never sleeps.

When wakeful at two in the morning
    I vow with all beings
to light incense and sit on my cushion—
it's time that I really wake up.

———

When I feel I haven't got time
    I vow with all beings
to light incense, and making my bows,
touch the place of no time.

———

When feelings build upon feelings
    I vow with all beings
not to be drawn from the Dharma:
"To nourish, not to indulge."

When anger or sadness arises
    I vow with all beings
to accept my emotional nature—
it's how I embody the Tao.

————

When anger raises my voice
    I vow with all beings
to take the hand of the other
and conspire in silence for a while.

————

When anger threatens my reason
    I vow with all beings
to wait while the storm runs its course
before poking my nose outside.

Whenever I'm feeling regretful
    I vow with all beings
to encourage myself by remembering
there's nothing to matter at all.

———

When I catch myself blowing smoke
    I vow with all beings
to clean the air by confessing
the smoke doesn't cover my fear.

———

When fear seems overwhelming
    I vow with all beings
to face this last great barrier:
it's terror of death I feel.

When fear seems overwhelming
    I vow with all beings
to walk through this ancient valley
breathing Mu right to the end.

———

When fear seems overwhelming
    I vow with all beings
to relinquish even my fear
and die, once and for all.

———

When I'm left with nothing to say
    I vow with all beings
to rest content in the knowledge
there is really nothing to say.

When I'm left with nothing to say
    I vow with all beings
to return to Bassui's practice:
"Who is hearing that sound?"

—————

Whenever I'm feeling discouraged
    I vow with all beings
to remember how Ling-yun saw peach trees
bloom after thirty hard years.

—————

Whenever I'm feeling discouraged
    I vow with all beings
to take my cue from the thrushes
who sing to the gloomiest sky.

Hearing the crickets at night
     I vow with all beings
to keep my practice as simple—
just over and over again.

———

Hearing the crickets at night
     I vow with all beings
to find my place in the harmony
crickets enjoy with the stars.

———

When geckos cry in the attic
     I vow with all beings
to return to myself and my practice
here in my intimate home.

When birdsong is loud in the trees
    I vow with all beings
to put down my work and to listen,
recreated as song.

———

At the edge of a quiet pond
    I vow with all beings
to settle myself as calmly
and nurture my duckweed and snails.

———

On the bank of a quiet stream
    I vow with all beings
to forget myself in this murmur—
my Gatha of Purification.

On the shore of the ocean at sunrise
    I vow with all beings
to rejoin this enormous power
that rises and falls in great peace.

———

Looking up at the sky
    I vow with all beings
to remember this infinite ceiling
in every room of my life.

———

When the day gets hotter and hotter
    I vow with all beings
to return to the place of no weather
and enjoy the lovely hot sun.

When I stroll around in the city
    I vow with all beings
to notice how lichen and grasses
never give up in despair.

———

When I stroll around in the mountains
    I vow with all beings
to watch for the many announcements
of my kinship with bushes and deer.

———

Watching a spider at work
    I vow with all beings
to cherish the web of the universe:
touch one point and everything moves.

Watching dung beetles roll up their treasures
    I vow with all beings
to consider that we don't roll treasures—
we flush them away every day.

———

Watching ants clean up the kitchen
    I vow with all beings
to clean up the waste on my desk
and the leftover crumbs in my head.

———

Dusting and sweeping the house
    I vow with all beings
to venture into the cellar
and shoo all the demons and rats.

Preparing the garden for seeds
    I vow with all beings
to nurture the soil to be fertile
each spring for the next thousand years.

———

When green leaves turn in the wind
    I vow with all beings
to enjoy the forces that turn me
face up, face down on my stem.

———

When a car goes by late at night
    I vow with all beings
to remember the lonely bakers
who secretly nurture us all.

When a train rattles by at the crossing
 I vow with all beings
to remember my mother and father
and imagine their thoughts in the night.

————

Whenever the telephone rings
 I vow with all beings
to allow it to ring one more time
as I carefully breathe in and out.

————

When the traffic is bumper to bumper
 I vow with all beings
to move when the world starts moving
and rest when it pauses again.

When a tire blows out on the freeway
    I vow with all beings
to call up the one who can't wobble
and steady myself and my car.

———

When the racket can't be avoided
    I vow with all beings
to close my eyes for a moment
and find my treasure right there.

———

When I turn on the TV news
    I vow with all beings
to reflect on the unspoken Dharma:
the fleeting nature of life.

When a chopper clatters above
    I vow with all beings
to evoke the original silence
when I call to make my complaint.

———

When people praise me for something
    I vow with all beings
to return to my vegetable garden
and give credit where credit is due.

———

Pushing my cart through the market
    I vow with all beings
to welcome the spinach and onions
and rejoice in their servant the sun.

When the table is spread for a meal
    I vow with all beings
to accept each dish as an offering
that honors my ancient path.

———

When the soup is too pungent with pepper
    I vow with all beings
to smile at my hostess and sip it
and tell a long funny story.

———

Whenever I'm tempted to judge
    I vow with all beings
to remember we both have two nostrils
and the same implacable fate.

When someone is late for a meeting
    I vow with all beings
to give up the past and the future
and relax where nothing begins.

———

When things are an absolute mess
    I vow with all beings
to walk to the park with the children
and play games of the unchanging Tao.

———

When the law of the sandbox is broken
    I vow with all beings
to refer the case to the magistrate
who teaches infants the Tao.

When people argue the Dharma
	I vow with all beings
to show how they started with truth
and then wrecked it with extrapolation.

———

Accepting the fault of another
	I vow with all beings
to encourage the original talent
that endeavors to make itself known.

———

When I offer critical comments
	I vow with all beings
to be clear there's no one I'm blaming
for the error that somehow crept in.

When someone tears at the fabric
    I vow with all beings
to come forth with the voice of no-source
and show how it cannot be torn.

———

When offered meaningless sex
    I vow with all beings
to draw on my store of affection
and grace as I turn it down.

———

When people overreact
    I vow with all beings
to hold up the ancient mirror
and reflect their deeper concern.

When dissension comes up in the family
    I vow with all beings
to suggest we get in our loving—
who knows if we'll be here next month?

————

When I argue with someone I love
    I vow with all beings
to use this potent conjunction
for clearing our common ground.

————

When someone preaches false Dharma
    I vow with all beings
to begin my clarification
as though we were holding hands.

When someone questions the Dharma
    I vow with all beings
to affirm that very question
from the ground that both of us share.

———

When emptiness worries a student
    I vow with all beings
to suggest that if everything's empty
there's nothing to worry about.

———

When the hara preoccupies students
    I vow with all beings
to acknowledge its vital importance
along with the bladder and spleen.

On reading scholarly comments
    I vow with all beings
to open my mouth for potatoes
and let the thrushes explain.

———

When I'm tempted to lay it out clearly
    I vow with all beings
to remember the words of my betters:
"Explanation leads only to doubt."

———

If action must wait for satori
    I vow with all beings
to forget satori completely.
What a relief! Let's go home!

When someone speaks of no-self
  I vow with all beings
to be sure there is no contradiction—
the speaker is there after all.

————

When talk gets too philosophical
  I vow with all beings
to recall the challenge of Buddha:
"What is life? What is death? What is this?"

————

In telling the story of Buddha
  I vow with all beings
to set forth the task of lay students:
"Come home without leaving the world."

When someone inquires about Zen
    I vow with all beings
to begin my response by explaining
there's really no doctrine at all.

———

When tempted to speak of attainment
    I vow with all beings
to recall there's no room for the timeless
in constructions of loss and gain.

———

If someone sees into the future
    I vow with all beings
to acknowledge as well the athlete
riding two horses at once.

When people discuss astral walking
    I vow with all beings
to admit to my own inclination
to wander about in my head.

———

If someone does something self-centered
    I vow with all beings
to mention whoever is missing:
the spouse, the child, or the squirrels.

———

When I hear people say, "Let it happen,"
    I vow with all beings
to work toward making it happen—
if it doesn't, then that's how it goes.

Hearing talk of expedient means
    I vow with all beings
to explore the matter more fully
and learn what expedient means.

———

When I'm drawn to watch crime on TV
    I vow with all beings
to smile at my own little drama
and expose the killer of time.

———

When people talk about war
    I vow with all beings
to raise my voice in the chorus
and speak of original peace.

If the bomb goes up after all
    I vow with all beings
to remember my mother's assurance:
"Never you mind, it's all right."

———

If the bomb goes up at last
    I vow with all beings
to relinquish even the earth
to the unborn there all along.

———

Regarding national interest
    I vow with all beings
to show how conventional wisdom
is not always common sense.

When nations take their revenge
    I vow with all beings
to suggest that revenge springs from anguish—
perhaps we created that pain.

———

When the army holds a parade
    I vow with all beings
to sing pacifist songs with the children
of Minsk, Tel Aviv, and Fort Bragg.

———

When federal taxes are due
    I vow with all beings
to refuse any role in the killing
of Sesshu, Dostoevsky, and Bach.

With jungles and oceans in danger
    I vow with all beings
to return to my zazen practice
and settle there right in the way.

————

With jungles and oceans in danger
    I vow with all beings
to suggest that interdependence
is the Way, as the Buddha maintained.

————

With tropical forests in danger
    I vow with all beings
to raise hell with the people responsible
and slash my consumption of trees.

With resources scarcer and scarcer
    I vow with all beings
to reduce my gear in proportion
even to candles and carts.

———

With resources scarcer and scarcer
    I vow with all beings
to consider the law of proportion:
my *have* is another's *have-not*.

———

When I reach for the keys to my car
    I vow with all beings
to consider alternate transport:
feet, or a bike, or the bus.

When a public utility fails
    I vow with all beings
to take up the obvious challenge—
it's time that we planted more beans.

———

Raking the leaves from my yard
    I vow with all beings
to compost extraneous thoughts
and cultivate beans of the Tao.

———

Watching gardeners label their plants
    I vow with all beings
to practice the old horticulture
and let plants identify me.

When feeling some inkling of progress
    I vow with all beings
to move on from this smoky condition—
even sparks aren't genuine fire.

———

When feeling some inkling of progress
    I vow with all beings
to remember how Chao-chou delighted
in progress for one hundred years.

———

At the point where everything vanishes
    I vow with all beings
to hurry along to my teacher
and see if there's anything left.

When I cry with the voice of the pheasant
    I vow with all beings
to hurry along to my teacher
and see if I'm really in tune.

———

When I cry with the voice of the pheasant
    I vow with all beings
to light incense and bow to the Buddha
and his sacred coincident world.

———

When I cry with the voice of the pheasant
    I vow with all beings
to come forth from my lapse and rekindle
my practice of voices and vows.

When I read about levels of insight
    I vow with all beings
to return the book to the bookcase.
"Oh bosh," as Grandma would say.

———

On reading the words of Ta-hui
    I vow with all beings
not to diminish my betters
who lived to the point long ago.

———

On reading the words of Thoreau
    I vow with all beings
to cherish our home-grown sages
who discern the perennial way.

Meeting somebody clear about karma
     I vow with all beings
to drop my chatter and scribble—
my long-sought teacher has come.

———

Drawing my lineage chart
     I vow with all beings
to be true to the timeless Buddha
and my teachers back through time.

———

Drawing my lineage chart
     I vow with all beings
to be true to the planet Venus
and her students, the grasses and deer.

Watching the stars after midnight
    I vow with all beings
to remember the point of existence
has no dimension at all.

———

Falling asleep at last
    I vow with all beings
to enjoy the dark and the silence
and rest in the vast unknown.

———

When Buddha appears in a dream
    I vow with all beings
not to deny or dismiss it—
my authentic dream in a dream.

When Buddha appears in a dream
    I vow with all beings
to take heart at this deep revelation
of the ancient, the timeless for me.

————

When roosters crow before dawn
    I vow with all beings
to acknowledge each voice in the chorus,
there you are, there you are, friend.

Acknowledgments

I begin my acknowledgments with nine bows to the geniuses of the *Hua-yen* and the *Avatamsaka* sutras. I am also indebted to and influenced by R. H. Blyth and his *Senryu: Japanese Satirical Verses*,[1] Shido Munan and his *Doka* ("Songs of the Tao"),[2] J. V. Cunningham and his aphoristic poetry,[3] and Peter Maurin and his *Easy Essays*.[4]

My teacher, Yamada Koun Roshi, guided me through koan study, the practice of seeing into succinct and potent presentations of fundamental matters, and I am endlessly grateful to him. Thich Nhat Hanh encouraged me to write gathas, as he does all his students and Buddhist friends. His own gathas are greatly helpful to me and to other students of meditation.[5]

I thank my students who encouraged me to persevere, especially Gil Fronsdal, who clarified the function of Buddhist vows for me after I thought I understood everything, and Carl Varady for his useful editorial suggestions. Also, I thank Augusto

Alcalde and members of the Vimalakirti Sangha in Cordoba, Argentina, who fed me and gave me the desk and leisure I needed to write the first draft.

Finally, I thank my wife and editor, Anne Hopkins Aitken. She keeps me sane and coherent with her loving encouragement, her practical assistance, and her cogent criticism.

NOTES

1. R. H. Blyth, *Senryu: Japanese Satirical Verses* (Tokyo: Hokuseido Press, 1949).
2. Tōrei Enji, *The Life of Shidō Munan*, trans. by Sōkaku Kobori and N. A. Waddell, in *The Eastern Buddhist: New Series* 2.1 (June 1970); Shidō Munan, *Sokushinki (Descriptions of the Mind)*, trans. by Kobori and Waddell, in Waddell, *The Eastern Buddhist* 2.2 and 3.2.
3. J. V. Cunningham, *The Collected Poems and Epigrams* (Chicago: The Swallow Press, n.d.).
4. Peter Maurin, *Radical Catholic Thought: Easy Essays* (West Hamlin, WV: Green Revolution, 1971).
5. Thich Nhat Hanh, *Being Peace* (Berkeley: Parallax Press, 1987), 5, 22, 66, 105. Also his *The Sun My Heart* (Berkeley: Parallax Press, 1988), 14–15.

Glossary

Bassui Tokushō (1327–1387). Japanese Zen Buddhist master whose students included many lay people.

Buddha. Shākyamuni, the historical Buddha (463?–383? B.C.E.); (Sanskrit) Enlightened One; nature of the universe and its beings; any being; title of several figures in the Buddhist pantheon.

Buddha-Tao (Sanskrit-Chinese). The Way or teaching of the historical Buddha and his successors; Dharma; Buddhism; the eightfold path; the Way apparent in the universe.

Ch'an (Chinese, Zen in Japanese). Meditation; harmony of the universal and the particular; Ch'an (Zen) Buddhist sect.

Chao-chou Ts'ung-shen (778–897). Long-lived Chinese Ch'an Buddhist master, source of the kōan Mu.

Dāna (Sanskrit). Charity; genenosity; relinquishment.

Dharma (Sanskrit). Religious, secular, or natural law; the law of karma; phenomena; Tao or Way; Buddhist teaching; the void.

Hakuin Ekaku (1686–1769). Japanese Zen Buddhist master and painter who reorganized Rinzai Zen procedures and teaching.

Hara (Japanese). Lower abdomen, considered to be the source of strength in formal Zen practice.

Interdependence. Everything depends on everything else, as the Buddha pointed out.

Interview. Dokusan or sanzen (Japanese), the private dialogue of teacher and student during formal Zen practice.

Karma (Sanskrit). Action; cause and effect; affinity (distinguish from fate).

Kōan (Japanese). Universal/particular; a presentation of the harmony of the universal and the particular; a theme of zazen to be made clear.

Kuan-yin (Chinese). Also Kuan-shih-yin (Kannon or Kanzeon in Japanese); One Who Hears Sounds (of the World); archetypal bodhisattva of mercy.

Ling-yün Chih-ch'in (ninth century). Chinese Ch'an Buddhist master, remembered especially for his realization at long last on seeing distant peach trees in bloom.

Mañjushrī (Sanskrit). Beautiful Virtue; archetypal bodhisattva of wisdom.

Middle Way. The Way of the Buddha, harmonizing the universal and the particular and other rational opposites; the eightfold path.

Mu (Japanese, Wu in Chinese). No; does not have; usually the first kōan of Zen practice, from case one of the *Wu-men kuan* (*Mumonkan* in Japanese, *The Gateless Barrier*).

Path. See Tao and Dharma.

Refuge. Ceremony expressing acceptance of the Three Treasures: Buddha, Dharma, and Sangha.

Samantabhadra (Sanskrit). Pervading Goodness; archetypal bodhisattva of great action (in conveying the Buddha Way).

Sangha (Sanskrit). Aggregate; priesthood; Buddhist fellowship; kinship of all beings.

Satori (Japanese). Enlightenment; the experience or condition of enlightenment. Compare kenshō (Japanese), seeing into true nature, a term limited to the experience.

Sesshin (Japanese). To touch (receive and convey) the mind. The Zen Buddhist retreat of five to seven days.

Sesshū Tōyō (1420–1506). Zen Buddhist priest and foremost Japanese ink painter.

Shidō Munan (1603–1676). Japanese Zen Buddhist master and poet.

Ta-hui Tsung-kao (1089–1163). Chinese Ch'an Buddhist master whose students included many lay people.

Tao (Chinese, distinguish from the Tao of Taoism). Way; Dharma, Buddha Way or Teaching; the eightfold path.

Way. See Tao and Dharma.

Wheel of the Dharma. Function or process of enlightenment in the world.

Zazen (Japanese). Seated meditation; formal Zen Buddhist practice.

Zen (Japanese pronuciation of Ch'an). Meditation; harmony of the universal and the particular; Zen Buddhist sect.

Zendō (Japanese). Meditation hall; Zen Buddhist center.

Index of Occasions for Practice

About the Author

Robert Aitken was one of the most prominent, influential, and highly esteemed Zen masters of the last fifty years. He was of seminal importance in shaping the expression of modern American Zen and, as one of the original founders of the Buddhist Peace Fellowship, was also a leading social activist advocating for social justice of all varieties. He is the author of numerous books on Zen Buddhism, including *Zen Master Raven*. He died in 2010.